Hope you enjoy your stay.

Please sign our guest book.

Thank you.

DATE

NAME

COMMENT:

DATE

NAME

COMMENT:

DATE

NAME

COMMENT:

DATE

NAME

COMMENT:

DATE

NAME

COMMENT:

DATE

NAME

COMMENT:

DATE

NAME

COMMENT:

DATE

NAME

COMMENT:

DATE

NAME

COMMENT:

DATE

NAME

COMMENT:

DATE

NAME

COMMENT:

DATE

NAME

COMMENT:

DATE

NAME

COMMENT:

DATE

NAME

COMMENT:

DATE

NAME

COMMENT:

DATE

NAME

COMMENT:

DATE

NAME

COMMENT:

DATE

NAME

COMMENT:

DATE	NAME

COMMENT:

DATE	NAME

COMMENT:

DATE	NAME

COMMENT:

DATE

NAME

COMMENT:

DATE

NAME

COMMENT:

DATE

NAME

COMMENT:

DATE

NAME

COMMENT:

DATE

NAME

COMMENT:

DATE

NAME

COMMENT:

DATE

NAME

COMMENT:

DATE

NAME

COMMENT:

DATE

NAME

COMMENT:

DATE

NAME

COMMENT:

DATE

NAME

COMMENT:

DATE

NAME

COMMENT:

DATE

NAME

COMMENT:

DATE

NAME

COMMENT:

DATE

NAME

COMMENT:

DATE	NAME

COMMENT:

DATE	NAME

COMMENT:

DATE	NAME

COMMENT:

DATE

NAME

COMMENT:

DATE

NAME

COMMENT:

DATE

NAME

COMMENT:

DATE

NAME

COMMENT:

DATE

NAME

COMMENT:

DATE

NAME

COMMENT:

DATE

NAME

COMMENT:

DATE

NAME

COMMENT:

DATE

NAME

COMMENT:

DATE	NAME

COMMENT:

DATE	NAME

COMMENT:

DATE	NAME

COMMENT:

DATE

NAME

COMMENT:

DATE

NAME

COMMENT:

DATE

NAME

COMMENT:

DATE	NAME

COMMENT:

DATE	NAME

COMMENT:

DATE	NAME

COMMENT:

DATE

NAME

COMMENT:

DATE

NAME

COMMENT:

DATE

NAME

COMMENT:

DATE	NAME

COMMENT:

DATE	NAME

COMMENT:

DATE	NAME

COMMENT:

DATE

NAME

COMMENT:

DATE

NAME

COMMENT:

DATE

NAME

COMMENT:

DATE

NAME

COMMENT:

DATE

NAME

COMMENT:

DATE

NAME

COMMENT:

DATE	NAME

COMMENT:

DATE	NAME

COMMENT:

DATE	NAME

COMMENT:

DATE	NAME

COMMENT:

DATE	NAME

COMMENT:

DATE	NAME

COMMENT:

DATE

NAME

COMMENT:

DATE

NAME

COMMENT:

DATE

NAME

COMMENT:

DATE

NAME

COMMENT:

DATE

NAME

COMMENT:

DATE

NAME

COMMENT:

DATE

NAME

COMMENT:

DATE

NAME

COMMENT:

DATE

NAME

COMMENT:

DATE

NAME

COMMENT:

DATE

NAME

COMMENT:

DATE

NAME

COMMENT:

DATE

NAME

COMMENT:

DATE

NAME

COMMENT:

DATE

NAME

COMMENT:

DATE

NAME

COMMENT:

DATE

NAME

COMMENT:

DATE

NAME

COMMENT:

DATE

NAME

COMMENT:

DATE

NAME

COMMENT:

DATE

NAME

COMMENT:

DATE

NAME

COMMENT:

DATE

NAME

COMMENT:

DATE

NAME

COMMENT:

DATE

NAME

COMMENT:

DATE

NAME

COMMENT:

DATE

NAME

COMMENT:

DATE

NAME

COMMENT:

DATE

NAME

COMMENT:

DATE

NAME

COMMENT:

DATE

NAME

COMMENT:

DATE

NAME

COMMENT:

DATE

NAME

COMMENT:

DATE

NAME

COMMENT:

DATE

NAME

COMMENT:

DATE

NAME

COMMENT:

DATE

NAME

COMMENT:

DATE

NAME

COMMENT:

DATE

NAME

COMMENT:

DATE	NAME

COMMENT:

DATE	NAME

COMMENT:

DATE	NAME

COMMENT:

DATE

NAME

COMMENT:

DATE

NAME

COMMENT:

DATE

NAME

COMMENT:

DATE

NAME

COMMENT:

DATE

NAME

COMMENT:

DATE

NAME

COMMENT:

DATE

NAME

COMMENT:

DATE

NAME

COMMENT:

DATE

NAME

COMMENT:

DATE

NAME

COMMENT:

DATE

NAME

COMMENT:

DATE

NAME

COMMENT:

DATE

NAME

COMMENT:

DATE

NAME

COMMENT:

DATE

NAME

COMMENT:

DATE

NAME

COMMENT:

DATE

NAME

COMMENT:

DATE

NAME

COMMENT:

DATE

NAME

COMMENT:

DATE

NAME

COMMENT:

DATE

NAME

COMMENT:

DATE	NAME

COMMENT:

DATE	NAME

COMMENT:

DATE	NAME

COMMENT:

DATE

NAME

COMMENT:

DATE

NAME

COMMENT:

DATE

NAME

COMMENT:

DATE	NAME

COMMENT:

DATE	NAME

COMMENT:

DATE	NAME

COMMENT:

DATE

NAME

COMMENT:

DATE

NAME

COMMENT:

DATE

NAME

COMMENT:

DATE	NAME

COMMENT:

DATE	NAME

COMMENT:

DATE	NAME

COMMENT:

DATE

NAME

COMMENT:

DATE

NAME

COMMENT:

DATE

NAME

COMMENT:

DATE

NAME

COMMENT:

DATE

NAME

COMMENT:

DATE

NAME

COMMENT:

DATE

NAME

COMMENT:

DATE

NAME

COMMENT:

DATE

NAME

COMMENT:

DATE	NAME

COMMENT:

DATE	NAME

COMMENT:

DATE	NAME

COMMENT:

DATE

NAME

COMMENT:

DATE

NAME

COMMENT:

DATE

NAME

COMMENT:

DATE

NAME

COMMENT:

DATE

NAME

COMMENT:

DATE

NAME

COMMENT:

DATE

NAME

COMMENT:

DATE

NAME

COMMENT:

DATE

NAME

COMMENT:

DATE

NAME

COMMENT:

DATE

NAME

COMMENT:

DATE

NAME

COMMENT:

DATE

NAME

COMMENT:

DATE

NAME

COMMENT:

DATE

NAME

COMMENT:

DATE

NAME

COMMENT:

DATE

NAME

COMMENT:

DATE

NAME

COMMENT:

DATE

NAME

COMMENT:

DATE

NAME

COMMENT:

DATE

NAME

COMMENT:

DATE

NAME

COMMENT:

DATE

NAME

COMMENT:

DATE

NAME

COMMENT:

DATE

NAME

COMMENT:

DATE

NAME

COMMENT:

DATE

NAME

COMMENT:

DATE

NAME

COMMENT:

DATE

NAME

COMMENT:

DATE

NAME

COMMENT:

DATE

NAME

COMMENT:

DATE

NAME

COMMENT:

DATE

NAME

COMMENT:

DATE

NAME

COMMENT:

DATE

NAME

COMMENT:

DATE

NAME

COMMENT:

DATE

NAME

COMMENT:

DATE

NAME

COMMENT:

DATE

NAME

COMMENT:

DATE

NAME

COMMENT:

DATE

NAME

COMMENT:

DATE

NAME

COMMENT:

CPSIA information can be obtained
at www.ICGtesting.com
Printed in the USA
BVHW091044050821
613729BV00004B/689